Enchantment

Enchantment

Poems of Awe from America's First Dude Ranch

SD Stalzer

Foreword by Liz Sanborn

Enchantment: Poems of Awe from America's First Dude Ranch
© 2023 Steven David Stalzer
ISBN 9798987731406

"The Stick Horse" and "Rope and Arrow" icons are used with permission from Eatons' Ranch.
Sunrise and deer icons designed by Lindy Gifford.
All interior photographs by the author, except where noted.
Cover scene photograph by Steven David Stalzer.
Cover inset photograph and back cover photos by Rosa Stalzer.

Steven David Stalzer, publisher
Edited by Genie Dailey
Cover and book design by Lindy Gifford, ManifestIdentity
Printed in the United States of America

For my Dad, Edwin,
who put me on my first horse
and convinced me I could ride anywhere.

And the big planets hanging—
I turned

Stumbling in a fever of a dream, down towards
The dark woods, from the kindling tops,

And came to the horses.

—Ted Hughes, "The Horses,"
from *The Hawk in the Rain* (1958)

CONTENTS

HORSES & HANDS

Foreword

Eatons' Ranch—those two words have a special place in my heart and the hearts of thousands of guests who have visited "America's First Dude Ranch." Nestled in the Big Horn Mountains on over 7,000 acres of astonishing Wyoming beauty, Eatons' Ranch is a land of rugged wonders—a true wilderness that includes mountains, streams, shrub-steppe, forest, and pasture. Since its inception, five generations of the Eaton family have been stewards of this beautiful land and have provided a magical experience for their guests that is rare in the fast-paced world we live in.

The ranch was started in 1879 by three brothers—Howard, Alden, and Willis. Originally located in North Dakota, the ranch moved to Wolf, Wyoming, in 1904 to accommodate its expanding dude ranch business. Wyoming offered their guests a more varied landscape for riding and plenty of pasture for their cattle operation. What began as Howard's passion for taking his friends on pack trips to the newly founded Yellowstone National Park became a living history of dude ranching in the American West.

I consider myself lucky to have discovered Eatons' Ranch in 1998. Recently divorced, I visited the ranch for a week of riding to try to catch a glimpse of the person I used to be, and to reconnect with what I had lost. I have always had a love of horses, and this proved to be one of the best decisions I have ever made. Little did I know when I embarked on that first journey that my life would be forever altered by my time at the ranch and by the lifelong friendships I have developed with both guests of the ranch and the Eaton family. I returned home from that first visit with a renewed sense of hope and a longing for vast open spaces where the world made sense to me. Like many "dudes" who have visited over the years,

Eatons' Ranch cast a spell on me that has continued unbroken for over twenty-five years.

I first met Steve (SD) Stalzer several years ago at the ranch when he was visiting with his family. I have had the privilege of becoming his friend and witnessing the magic of the ranch through his eyes as well as my own. We have spent eight years watching our families connect through shared experiences and adventures. Whether an all-day ride into the Big Horn Mountains, a hike to a hidden swimming hole, or a quiet moment on the trail with a great horned owl, Eatons' Ranch never disappoints and always leaves us moved by the glory of the land and a legacy that shares its treasures with so many grateful guests.

When Steve told me he was writing a book of poetry about the ranch and the surrounding area, I was delighted. I cannot think of a more fitting form of expression for this special place. Steve's poetry narrates a moving experience of reverence and connection that is common among visitors to the American West. Full of sensual detail and philosophical wanderings, *Enchantment* captures the majesty, natural history, and awe of Wyoming and the ranch—from the immensity of the mountains to the trust found in a sure-footed horse.

Whether you enjoy riding or just love vast open spaces, my hope for you is to discover, through these pages, a piece of yourself long forgotten. A brief respite from this overfilled world. A chance to stop, breathe, listen. To see anew what has been in front of you all along. The awesome beauty that can be found in the smallest details—a horse's nuzzle, an alpine flower, a fox kit's playful spirit. It is the small things in life that give our lives meaning, if only we take notice of them.

Liz Sanborn

Introduction

If you've ever been on a horse, you know how mounting it immediately settles you into the present moment. Somehow, being responsible for a thousand pounds of muscle with a will of its own forces all other thoughts out of your mind as you remind yourself to sit properly and recall the basics of steering. And with that new mindfulness, that special presence between human and animal, a door opens to experiences of awe. Awe of the new directions in which you can literally take yourself. Awe of your own strengths as you conquer your fears. Awe of the pristine mountains, abundant wildlife, and geologic history which remind you of your small place. An awakening of a longing often forgotten—for freedom, for memory, for being at one with the movements of the earth.

As a family from the East Coast of the United States, we first immersed ourselves in the awe of the American West by visiting a dude ranch (a western vacation experience with a century of history). I think we were about an hour and a half into our first day at Eatons' Ranch in Wolf, Wyoming, when one of my kids asked, "Can we come back here?" Children have an uncanny ability to perceive what often, as adults, we miss. It was clear to her, looking around at the barn, the horses, the evening light, the communal dining hall with its friendly faces, that this place would cast a spell on us, and that we'd return again and again. She was right. As I write this, we are preparing for our eighth consecutive summer visit as "serial dudes." Every year, we mark our children's changes: in acceptance of new people and new ways, in self-confidence as they ride off with friends to experience their own adventures and write their own tales.

This enchantment is a common experience at the ranch. It is not unusual for us to meet multigenerational families returning to the ranch annually for their third or fourth decade. A place of wonder where time slows down, encouraging you to leave behind the to-do lists and feed on history and endless beauty, is a potion for uniting again with one's heart. As I write in the poem, "On the Ancient Porch," at the ranch "time catches like my foot / tripping on a well-placed root / disrupting my hurried walk / to listen to yesterday speak."

The poems and photos in this collection attempt to capture some of the reverence of this experience. The chapter called "Journeys" is drawn from a set of excursions on the ranch and trips to other sites within Wyoming. "Encounters" focuses on the vast abundance of the natural world in Wyoming, from wildflowers to elk and more. "Horses & Hands" contains tributes and moments of gratitude for the ranch operations and its incredibly talented and dedicated staff. The Glossary shares some explanations of the more uncommon words and references used within the book.

There is something about being able to ride in any direction your heart desires that brings you back to yourself, allows you to let go of unnecessary mental chatter, and reconnects you with your inner world. Readers will find nuggets of reflection inspired by watchfulness and witness throughout these pages. I hope this book encourages you to reunite with your own heart and inspires your own contemplation of the things that fill you with awe.

SD Stalzer
2023

JOURNEYS

Solstice

The great sky inhales, still as 6 a.m. glass,
plains a seabed lapping against graven mountains,
my sense of distance in each direction
fractured and uncertain,
my trusty Wiggins under me, a fine horse, well-trained,
his sure-footed steps securing me to the trail.

His slick coat sweats in the June heat,
his panting underneath me responding to my urge
to take me upward to a higher place,
to view the Ten Thousand Things great and small.

Up we climb, dry air in our nostrils,
red dust of rainless weeks in motion,
plumes from the Triassic
freed after 200 million years,
yarrow, lupine, and Indian paintbrush
scattered across the grassy hillsides
by the hand of a nameless artist.

Above the rise, a sandstone spine snakes
its vertebral remains,
an extinct sea pushed upward in faults,
weather-worn,

exposed outcroppings of primeval times a message
from lives lived before humanity's dawn.

I feel the solstice upon us,
endless days marking the tenuous web
of the living and the dead in balance—

bison herds molting their winter coats,
wolf pups and bear cubs, and mountain goat kids alive at last,
the trout under the watchful eye of the eagle,
fossilized bones rebirthed in exposed rock,
mud pots and hot springs and geysers
recycling the ever-flowing river of existence.

What lessons do you have for us, ancestors of the earth?
What stories rise from the soil at your urging?

Pinned against the press of progress,
this moment, immobilized, embraces me,
an urgent pulse sounding again and again:

I am here now.
I am
here now.
I am here.
Now.

In the Land of Giants

A litany of doubts bounce in my mind
as I realize just how alone I will be
on my first solo all-day,
no other rides scheduled out this way,
just my vulnerable memory
to guide my hand,
and my trust in a horse named Splinter.

Up we go past the red gate,
the precarious switchbacks dusty lightning
zigzagging back and forth—
it would be a long fall down. I breathe
and remind myself about horse skill,
what a luxury to slip a foot and still have three.

The obstacle survived, we stop
at Mile High Camp along the creek,
drawn to the crisp melody glancing off cliffs,
crows squeaking like children fingering
new clarinets, blowing a bit too hard.

On we ride into upland fields
as the trail reveals geological magic,
something like love rising inside as I recognize
the Madison limestone towering to the right—
a colossal old friend—

monument to countless creatures once swimming,
now transformed into giants,
their high foreheads governing their lands,
comforting my misgivings, their sandstone
mouths curved in the seriousness of elders,
full beards of balsam root, larkspur, and lupine
ranging as far as sight, a balm
to heal all tragic fears of night.

I dismount at the Missouri gate
to ingest their world with all senses,
whirling 360 degrees,
in this singular place where the sky
meets the movements of history
to pierce petty worries,
etched cliffs an open book
ready to be read
by those open to reading it.

The lambent sunlight ripples
on our damp shoulders,
the endless valley below us sweeping
into rusty side canyons and eroding badlands
where just yesterday I scrabbled
like a dung beetle in the clay,
oblivious to a council of giants
counseling me across scorched fields of hay.

Prairie Dog Town

In ones and twos they jump-yip
heads back flung airbound
missiles with a ringing chirp
as we ride into their dusty town
miles of burrows and cropped grass
no place for us to hide
in the bleaching sun.

Cartoonish rodents they stare
with black eyes their
coterie alerted to our slowing
spying a predator
on the loose knowing
we're more like sneaky coyotes
than yesterday's eagle attacking
with violence from above.

Petite ears pressed flat they stand
at attention on hind feet
stubby front paws folded
on camel hair chests
a posse of bowling pins
with bellies rounded
their message clear

yer kind ain't welcome here.

Shed Hunter
for Scot Sanborn

Swaying with his steed
back and forth
never taking the same path twice,
the shed hunter
explores the lonely route

eyes scanning left, scanning
the beige grasses to the right
for the telltale flash of white
an antler
lying in the parted plains or

prickly brush or between hills,
places not seen by ordinary folk
where a bull elk might rake trees
to impress the girls
or lock horns in battle.

Snaking to the left, hours
spent searching to the right—
another forked stick another
antelope bone—
praying

for a crown jeweled with sun-bleach,
coronation of a lost king
just one more, one
more to add to his collection
(so many you could fill a small barn)

he weaves around exposed
outcrops and down the hollow
haunted by an old elk once seen
maybe fallen near here,
an imperial if luck is with him

skull and antlers still attached
waiting to be discovered
by his persistent eye—
what joy to be
the first to hold it.

in the beginning: water
Shape Poem

we trot along the worn track,
silty badlands, mounds of shaped
shale rising in loitering waves, harry
the horse watching over us from his
grave, our kids pushing us forward
into an eager lope. freedom—

the silver thread of human to
horse to each other to ground
to open space—binds us as one
as we run to indian rock, an annual
favorite, easy ride with an easy view.

how many riders have passed here,
felt the thirsty air smiling across
faces and hair, a flicker of
expanding exhilaration
growing warmer
with each step?

how many guests have
wondered as we do now
about how it came to be,
about how it all still is?

we pass through
the white gate, a pair
of mule deer watching
with ears up, alert sonar
scanning us for friendliness
as we reach the knoll, a sand-
stone outcrop, and recall
the interior seaway that
wandered through
here, connecting

the gulf of mexico
to the arctic over 65
million years ago, the
ancient ocean inundating
a thousand miles of future
grasslands with evolving life,
memories of its distant reign
preserved as hardened sand
dunes, frozen undulations
surrendered to the pitting
of windy rain, petrified
heirlooms a reminder
of our cellular past.

The Time of Splitting Fishes

Kemmerer, WY

The dialed-up sun irons shirts into our backs
as we bend over rocks
splitting fishes

imagining when this landscape
was a deep ancient lake
unobserved hum of insects
       smells of hot decay
in undisturbed state

humid forest on subtropic coastline
schools of fish at the end of the line
mass mortalities of oxygen deprivation
drifting to the bottom of the basin
frozen in time
no bacteria for decomposition
just fine-grained mud
preserving their position
laminating
layers like
      plywood.

Prey lie with their predators in the murky low light
toothy Diplomystus with his underbite

dinner still inside his jaws
the successful bowfin
unchanged without flaws

freshwater stingray in undulating flight
long before human feet scraped across the land
without interest or desire
to understand
what mysteries lie beneath.

With hammer and chisel we descend
greedy children with eager eyes
to split open the package
searching for the prize

between fine layers of nature's fine art
tap
   tap
      tap
to chip them apart

carefully removing fragile rock
that desiccates our hands
searching for fish fossils
from ancient lands

preserved in pressured residues
my son attacks the beige hues

to find two Knightia three inches long
their death dance intermingled
like birdsong
ribs and taut skin still intact
their spines and delicate fins
       uncracked

resurrected from chalky lime
unblinking eye sockets
look through us
'cross time.

We examine his discovery
of evolutionary bones
brown and white photographs
in fifty-million-year stone

spellbound by the opened book
       earthbound
we take a deeper look
and consider a world without us
in the time of splitting fishes.

somehow you thought you were stuck

that the things you came
into this world with
were all you had
the ability to think
through the problem
the way you could scrape
together an answer
from just little bits
of bare schooling
quiet mouth that watched
everyone with shyness
until you had the one safe
thing to say

until courage
that galloping heart
pried your lips open
with words of defiance
even though you were told
to keep your mouth shut
even though you knew
your reward
for lips pried open
might be a fistful of schoolboys
some thursday afternoon

until one day you
stood on the box
and climbed into the saddle
and you realized
that nose-to-tail
all ends up in the same place
and you noticed
that he'd listen
most of the time
to your gentle rein on his neck
and that in fact
you could ride
in any direction
without limits.

One Tenuous Step

This rutted road diverges again,
an unexpected spur trail appearing ahead
like a reflection on the horizon,
            a mirage quivering,
unclear and unformed.

The sinewy tendrils
of another change,
a choice to make,
its rewards and idiosyncrasies
still nascent in imagination.

A cortisol rush
of fear and excitement
wraps itself around my chest.

How many times
I've trudged this dirt,
my face to the un-
even ground,
watching the grasses
underfoot, unaware
of game trails just
outside my periphery.

I breathe deeply
to calm the palpitations,
the hidden way
         rising

like a response to
the true heart's invocation,
the path
a creation of the Maker
at play.

One
tenuous
step
off
the road
embraces
another.

How to Avoid Falling into a Cauldron
Yellowstone National Park

You will see the steam of desire rising
before it even shimmies into consciousness,
dragon's breath billowing,
concentric rings of bubbling fire
entering you to hum along nerve pathways
as you approach her on the narrow boardwalk,
signs everywhere warning you to look not touch,
to stay on the prescribed path.

Her malachite waters will sing to you,
her endless layers of cerulean power offered just to you,
her magma heart miles below
encircling acidic waters heated well beyond boiling,
exhaling curious sulfur spells
that make mountains
and destroy them, tempting you
with etched white diamonds
and gold enriched sands
where even bears hesitate to walk.

You'll want to draw closer, ignoring the signs,
to gently walk on thin crust—
at your age, your need to see yourself recycled
into a new story so strong
you'd shrug off self-preservation
to stand on the edge for a selfie:
proof that youthful gods
have not yet abandoned you.

Your family might watch from a distance,
horrified when you lose your footing
as she pulls you into herself,
your skin dissolving in seconds,
and then your muscles,
and with them your regrets.

The rangers might close the park to
try to recover what they can of you.

All they would find are your two
crystalline heart bones.

ENCOUNTERS

Photo by Liz Sanborn

Katydid

after Mary Oliver, "The Sun"

Have I ever seen anything in my life
more wonderful
than the way this katydid

a sugar snap pea
green as the spring grape,
hoists herself up my window

first her short right arm
with its grapple hook reaching up,
sensing her surroundings

then her middle limb,
followed by enormous
catapulting hind legs stilting her upward

antennae two curved whips
covered in receptors to help her see
in the late summer dark?

Studied face to the glass
with little whiskery barbs,
her nose wiggles up and down to find a path,

stopping now and then
to reach a fist to her mouth
hoping to taste a trace of bitter leaf

an aphid or small bug
perhaps, some tiny
insect eggs or desiccated
remains of the day.

What turn of grace assembled
hearing organs on her legs,
gifted her with night sense
and a song of incrimination—
"Katy did, Katy did it!"
as she rubs her forewings together
in a call of territorial warning?

What consequential turn
brought our little lives together
right now, when I needed
something to wonder about,
something to remind me
of what is real
in a world of power and things?

seduction

a tiny clutch of elk hair is my fiction
a thin wisp of filament my lifeline
connected through guides to
                     stiffened hands
praying for trout.

i am the canyon caddis
riding the current high my shadow
bobbing above slick muscles
        their arrows pulled back
hungry eyes taking aim.

just upstream the mended line
i float into agitated waters
          a precocious falsehood
cream wings standing erect with seduction
hackles languid on the surface tension
drifting drag-free past desire
stacked in the hidden pool.

watching. watching.

marmots

Tanka poem

yellow-bellied

             pups

chasing

      sun-washed ochre tails

rock den

               out of reach

careful

mother

watches

us

calculating eyes wary

wild peas

Tanka poem

roadside vines growing
squiggly with flying stems
animal-rooted
standing on one stretching foot
flamingo bonnets sunning

Wildfires (2020)

You can see the smoke from the horizon to the plains, veins of ochre sandstorm drifting from the west, obscuring the eternal yet ever-changing mountains from the heights of South Red Canyon. The acrimonious California wildfires shriek their way across the state, a gigafire eating an area greater than the size of Rhode Island. The largest wildfire season in recorded history, they say, started by impish thunderstorms playing with matches, their grievous mischief flinging lightning across drought-stricken patches of undergrowth which humbly accept their immolation. Stubby dead hands send wildlife and wild humans running headlong from the tip of the burning spear.

An inferno covering four million acres, its ash cloud of volcanic proportions, its visual distortions shutting out the sun, breathes its toxic exhalation into the jet stream. Infectious embers spread tree to tree like The Pandemic, but without the tools of personal protective equipment and social distancing to slow its progress.

Tangerine trails sail over the Bay Bridge, even as the air we breathe right here, thirteen hundred miles east on a knobby summit, tastes like pale dust—yet another reason to wear a mask during an already exhausting year that will take so much. I feel the slow shifting in my nose, an irritating tickle in the lungs like fear: not even a love affair as steadfast as this is safe from the greedy arms of a carbon-soaked atmosphere.

Horse Skull Resting in the Endless Grass

Horse skull resting in the endless grass,
servant fallen long ago,
runabout riders now passed,

Sutured cranium weathered white
by seasons of sun and snow,
dolomite in the midday light.

Flesh cleansed by vultures,
coyotes, and mice,
revealing a pristine sculpture,

chiseled alabaster,
evolutionary prize,
worked by the skills of a master.

When did your eyes last look back
to horsecakes in your saddlebags,
eager for a pat and well-earned snack?

What velvet muzzle
nuzzled mortal hands
as you dropped reins creekside
to rest sore muscles?

I trace your forehead, nostril to poll,
imagining your life before,
and wonder what stumble
caused your soul
to land here,
a meal for carnivores.

Photo by Liz Sanborn

Wapiti

Grasslands fading to flax and rust
twitching in the icy September wind,

a herd of wapiti rise from the mist,
eighty-five white rumps grazing,
migrated from mountains to plains to fatten—
the dominant bull elk, collector of cows,
standing alert,
his twelve-point rack a mighty headdress
magnifying his will.

Muscles shaped by hardship,
chocolate neck stretched out low,
oaken antlers fallen back
he sounds his metallic harmonic,
an other-worldly warning to all
who would challenge his imperative
to spread his genes far and wide.

Here and there he tends his harem,
a sharp nod to wandering stragglers,
trotting to the left to shape the herd,
a quick rush to disband young males
asserting their own instinctual voice.

Now he moves through the crowd,
striding to one cow, then another,
tongue flicking for permission,
a missionary of legacy,
evangelizing his creation

like the poet collecting words
sharpened for the next generation,
impregnating hearts with light
from a brief time of majesty.

treetops are painting

Tanka shape poem

bristle brush treetops
amaranth and amber fire
painting clouds with light
fog rising over the creek
this
fros-
ty
au-
tumn
mor-
ning

Wild Plums

Wild plums
discovered
with joy on
my foothills ride,
hiding in
scrub brush
off to the
side,

stunted,
unexpected
forage
on the slope,
attracting
wandering mule
deer
or antelope,

sign of autumn
tempting, I
dismount to
stretch my legs,
lean over to kiss
dusty
periwinkle
eggs.

Warning to a Black Bear

Your hearing,
seven times more sensitive
than a dog's,
must have alerted you—
you must have heard me
shushing up the gravel,
interrupting your chubby consideration
of our cabin perched on the creek,
reflecting almost as I would on
whether some peanut butter
and crackers
might be a happy digestive
after a diet of tree-masts, perhaps,
fallen forgotten in the grass;

or imagining
an open jam jar on the back porch,
familiar as your own black fur,
where we humans carry on
with gesticulating appendages
trailing crumbs and lost lids,
feeling safely unwatched,
unhiding ourselves from
bunkers of clapboard and stone.

I see you flirt with your options
in your language of tongue-clicks
and grunts—
creek bed an easy escape,
porch steps just three feet away—
slick bristles unmoving
as you seem to shrug at me
with a stare of satisfied survival.

Have you forgotten
that story of your kin—
candy bars playing in your mind—
the one who visited
just a bit too often? The one
whose musky body was
turned inside out
to decorate a wall with
lolling tongue and glass eyes,
a tale of forage gone wrong,
now watching us night after night
eat popcorn at the bar
with whiskey served up neat.

HORSES & HANDS

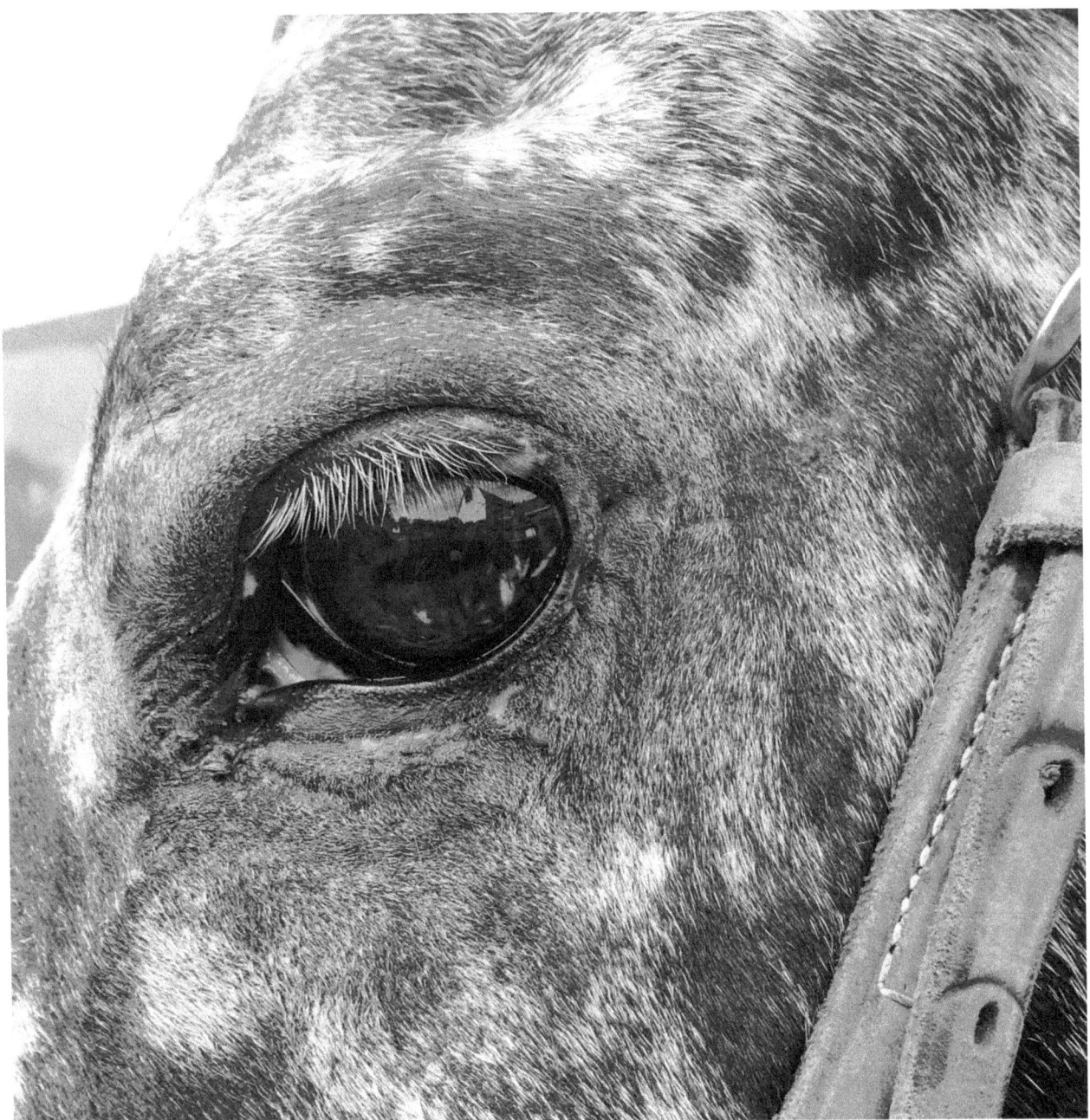

Photo by Rosa Stalzer

Wrangler Heartbeats

after Jericho Brown, "Duplex"

Wrangler hearts, the beat of the ranch
up before we've stirred from dreams—

dreams: a heaven of endless days—
wrangling horses from dusky pastures,

running them in angles of dusty twilight
up to the barn for the day's hot work.

They work the barn's signup list,
ninety names for the morning ride

ninety hearts to rope for ninety guests:
saddles, stirrups, cinches.

I get saddled, stirred up like a blind date,
my pinto's sizing eye a tentative flutter,

my stomach fluttering a tentative love,
grateful for reliable wrangler heartbeats.

How to Keep the Barn Happy

Sonnet, for Will Ferguson and Nate Schmeiser

In all your dealings, try to be polite,
It is expected in the Western way.
No need to speak so heated with a bite,
Be patient while you wait to mount your bay.
Remember all the work that goes behind
To get you ready for the morning ride,
The work to get your perfect horse assigned,
And trust that you won't need a wrangler guide.

When riding up the rocky and the sheer,
You'll let your horse determine his own pace,
Don't run him up or down the rocks, my dear,
And to the barn don't ever let him race.
Keep track of time, I cannot overstate,
Or learn the consequence of being late!

2019 flood

ripped-up root-wreck
debris   choking downstream
spring leaves rent from mother limbs
bank-sent   by joker hands

canyon faces land-sliding
   soil liquefaction
     washing out switchbacks
      leaving boulders like steer
sneering on blocked trails

powers torrent the unleashed snowpack
risen six feet over the bridge stacks
wood planks shattered
as scattered trout
          swim in bushes
footbridge kicked off its foundation
unprepared for vacation
no one crossing anytime anywhere

repairs sound their progress
hammer and saw attacking this
widespread   mess
high expectations arriving soon
disguised as discerning guests

           hurry

Lessons for Dudes

Eat a breakfast with coffee,
Eggs and sausage are fine.
Sign up for the morning ride.

Breathe in the clean mountain air,
Tightness gone from your chest,
Your horse rocking right and left.

Seeing in all directions,
Rise over the canyon.
Leave your work lists abandoned.

Your tribe of friends new and old
Sit for conversation.
Mind their great observations.

Like the trout sipping mayflies,
Welcome the perfect flow.
Time moves deliciously slow.

Joyful mem'ries fill your plate
With emotional food—
Simple lessons for a dude.

Horse Heads on the Rail

Saddled and ready to ride, my **horse heads** over to his peers. Gets tied **on**. Gets his reins wrapped over **the rail**. I wonder what sorts of thoughts he has. Do horses **question** the nature of their reality? Their work–life balance? Do they laugh at **us**? Our fragile fantasies **with** our heeled Ariat boots and wide-brimmed straw hats? He looks **wary** of my intentions. I **eye** him with the anticipation of an eager child and ask a wrangler **what's** his name. Jackal. Lean, wolf-like, clever. I consider **the plan** for our outing **today**, my first day back in the saddle, ready to ride again.

I'm **praying** to mountain gods that the **for**est will be as cool as **an** early morning twitter. Praying they will be **easy** on us on this risky **ride**. All rides at our own risk. Past the turnoff to **No**rth Red to those twitchy **switchbacks**. Once when my son was young, his horse butt-slid on that flat shale **or** loose gravel. We were so **sweaty** in the squinting sun, we didn't even notice him hanging on tight until our hearts stopped with the groaning clatter of rockslide. Practice and instinct gripping the reins. The practiced horse just getting **back** up. Like this was just any other day. Like he had already warned us.

Horse heads on the rail,
question us with wary eye—
what's the plan today?
Praying for an easy ride,
no switchbacks or sweaty back.

Photo by Rosa Stalzer

Enchantment

Sitting at the round table
with new friends from everywhere,
just arrived from our long drive
about an hour ago,
the sounds of sharing
filling the dining hall with daring stories
of the day, attended
by an elk head with generous rack
opened wide in welcome—
beef and vegetables not yet cold—
my daughter turns to me and asks,
"Can we come back here?"

Somehow she senses the onset
of an affair of new love
before I even touch the ground,
the way it rises up in your belly
ahead of your mind's certainty,
dusty heat washing away
every last doubt of the city,
purifying us
with the smell of horse and hay
like pheromones,
a sudden seduction by guttural attraction

to wooden cabins with cryptic names—
Nimick, Wigwam, Moss—
unchanged for decades.

Blindsided by the spell
of transfiguration, dissolving
shields of pressed pants
and stiff shirts
into cowboy hats and riding boots,
we trust in practiced beasts,
elvish ears rotating like radar,
who show us the way down
old creek beds up
shale washes
across windy
grass-rippled canyons—
an enchantment binding us
for at least a generation.

With Our Own Eyes

Gathering up the guests
to take to the hoof, a line
of docile horses, they know
the way to Domo's,
the promise of picnic tables and
the smoky memory of steaks
emptying the ranch in twos
and fours
as we loosen the rein
to traverse the plain
unhurried.

The light settles as muskmelon
and apricot across the mountains,
brushing rocks and badlands
with the orange spice of heaven,
like a Bierstadt painting, glorifying
the romance of an endless West
full of opportunity
and promise.

My eyes scan the canvas, and I
think of Howard, Willis, and Alden
exploring this broad expanse, gazing
with awe upon the exalted,

and what they must have felt on
their first visit here,
Creation,
sculpted by the hands of sun and rain,
grasslands flush with game,
mountains shape-shifting and limitless
which their hearts had to share
again
and again

first with a few friends,
then with dudes coming to ride,
now just a whisper urging us to see
the evening light
with our own eyes.

Enchantment

Rain

Listen
  to the giddy
    galloping
      lightly touching down

on this cabin's roof
  unshod hooves
    beating in fours
      circling the pasture

percussive patter
  slackening
    stiff shoulders
      as I lie in bed

given up to the day
  of recalcitrant rain
    imagining horses
      huddled in hayfields

wind-whipped withers
  without a dry blanket
    I pull the wool
      up to my cool nose

its leaden weight
  pushing my chest down
    into the fluttering nod
      of a distant doze.

On the Ancient Porch

I.

Wolf Creek breathes in a perfumed breeze,
shifting downstream across willow-green leaves,
bubbling, muttering,
head-voices left drowning,
the afternoon moving like the careful steps
of a horse coming down the pass,
its guest soon to be unsaddled.

Sheltered from the daily battle,
exhaling easy, slow,
my shoulders drop low,
bands returning to position,
stretched for too long through tough decisions
and the overuse of living.

II.

From the ancient porch high above the creek,
I hear the music of a world in relief,
a madrigal too beautiful to bear:
the sweet tenor of snowmelt
a cascading caress,
sizzling cicadas clicking like crabs
dressed by the warming sun,

the mocking birds' counterpoint
a sweet cacophony,
symphonic poem high in the canopy.

III.

Stripped of bark, three ancient logs,
the tan legs of a lover,
toned calves traced by hand,
support cross-pieced arms that hover
in the roof's embrace,
time travelers bearing weight and witness
for a century or more
to thousands of lives moving
across this wood-worn floor,
their memories exposing trails
on the silver gelatin print of time.

Here the dudes from
Pittsburgh, Chicago, New York,
rested from their daily strains,
pains left behind for adventure,
preparing their packs
for Yellowstone to see grizzlies,
and learn of their own insignificance,
planning day rides to Medicine Wheel
or Custer's final chance—

generations of visits framed
by children peering over the edge,
launching stick-boats to dance
on the waters below.

Here the guests of one hundred years
have left their ghosts,
their hosts recording lives paused
for a week or month or two,
nurtured by a low-altitude
jet stream throttled down,
grateful to fade
their pasts a trifle,
decelerating
to an easy float on a riffle.

IV.

The sun shimmers itself out
as the electric buzz rises,
a crescendo reinforcing
insistent insect lives,
today's finale on the creek,
and time catches like my foot
tripping on a well-placed root,
disrupting my hurried walk
to listen to yesterday speak.

Roping Competition

Ten thousand volts clang
through this tailgating crowd,
ringside echoes
exciting fantasies of riches, heavy bets
from last night's Calcutta auction
still murmuring in pockets,
and too much whiskey
still weighing on eyelids.

The sun's raw blind casts its mass
on our scalps as we shelter
in the shade of our F-250,
Mike's Lemonades in hand, ducking
heavy dust clouds ignited
by heavy hooves thundering
in the ninety-degree heat.

The chute man trips a lever and the steer bolts from the gate a thunderous charge of hoofs his head down with a pink head wrap around his horns tracing a straight line to the far end of the ring while a pair of riders chase in adrenaline-stoked pursuit the header getting aligned in precious seconds and throwing his rope catching a half-head and turning the steer to the left while the heeler aims for the hind legs trying to time her throw—but just missing her target as he trots casually off.

Next a pair of wranglers
well-loved by the staff, wizards
chiseled with the practice
of years, prepares
with careful coils
and balanced saddles, ready
to throw fire
and molten steel.

*The gate slams open and they take off after their quarry tossing dust
and dirt into the light breeze as all hearts race with the galloping
rhythm of the chase just five seconds this time a perfect hold across
both horns and the turn executing with precision as the heeler expertly
times the loop placing it just so the unlucky steer's legs step right in and
then pulling him up like an embarrassed rascal caught in escape—8.2
seconds of perfection nearly impossible to beat.*

In the midst of the spectators,
a group of young dishwashers
spring up and down,
clasping hands, screaming
heady excitement
(they pooled their resources
for this expensive bet),

now imagining their unlikely winnings,
crinkled green cash for
new boots or cowboy hats,

a night of fine liquor, relief
from the factory monotony of
scrape-soap-scrub-rinse-repeat
scrape-soap-scrub-rinse-repeat

—the relentless weight
of dishes and pans calling
like drill sergeants
from the steamy stainless fortress—

forgotten for a while
in the crazed sounds of the win.

Photo by Liz Sanborn

Horse Nation

Mitákuye Oyásìn ("All are related")

Full moon veiled in the midsummer night,
at dusk an inviting light,
compelled to see more clearly
I walk the gravel road,
to enter the hallowed hayfield
      seeking secrets revealed,
hidden in the matted grass.

The pewter disk still unseen,
paused in anticipation,
its aura tracing the abalone ridge—
I watch, bewitched,
the grasses changing to silver greens,
      metallic sheen
lengthening across the valley.

An earthquake rumble pulls my ears up,
pours horses into the field,
let out to pasture with wild-again glee,
loud whinnies calling with love to their friends
kyrrrrreeeeeee! kyrrrrreeeeeee!
("I am here!")
echoing from the rocks to the right,
streaming magic in all directions
into the deepening night.

Some head up the pass, others
run straight toward me as I leap aside
and press against the wire fence,
                         saved from myself,
heat and raw animal sense
radiating inward as they gallop past,
dark eyes penetrating me like black fire.

Encircling the pasture to dance
the sacred ceremony clockwise
in scattered clumps of earth,
          they prance,
manes trailing behind upturned heads,
flickering flames
moving as one
kyrrrrreeeeeee! kyrrrrreeeeeee!
transformed into gods of the plains:
"Holy Dogs"—
a gift from Beings of Thunder,
witnessed in wordless wonder.

The conjured moon emerges over the pass,
dipping my new family in platinum and brass,
a sense of calm settling on the field,
they yield to graze in twos and threes,
and welcome me with healing gaze
          into their Nation.

Glossary

Calcutta auction: open auction held in conjunction with a contest of multiple entrants, in which sequential bidding to "buy" a contestant or team commences across a randomly selected order of contestants or teams

Diplomystus: extinct genus of a freshwater fish distantly related to modern-day herrings and sardines, commonly found in the Green River Formation, a geologic formation of the Eocene Epoch (about 50 million years ago) spanning three basins in Colorado, Wyoming, and Utah

Domo: nickname for Bill Eaton's mother-in-law, Nannie Alderson; also refers to the old cabin where she lived in the 1920s

dude: visitor, often a city-dweller, vacationing on a ranch in the western US

Holy Dog: Lakota name for the horse, believed to have come as a gift from the Thunder Beings, and representing a connection to the spirit world

Knightia: extinct genus of a freshwater fish of the Eocene Epoch, and the official state fossil of Wyoming

liquefaction: in soil, the process whereby water saturation causes a loss in strength or cohesion, resulting in a solid with the properties of a liquid

Madison limestone: sequence of carbonate rocks deposited approximately 360–325 million years ago in the area of the Rocky Mountains and Great Plains

mast: fruit of forest trees and shrubs, such as acorns and other nuts

Missouri gate: a simple gate to pass through a wire fence, usually requiring unhooking a metal loop by hand

Mitákuye Oyásìn: Lakota phrase reflecting a worldview of the interconnectedness of all life

shape poem: also known as a concrete poem, is a form in which the layout of the words on the page reflect some physical aspect of the subject

shed: an antler that has fallen from a deer or elk as part of their normal growth process

tanka: free verse poem originating in Japan, consisting of five phrases where the 1st and 3rd contain 5 syllables, and the remaining contain 7 syllables

Ten Thousand Things: term from Taoist philosophy referring to the multitude and diversity of objects in the universe or natural world

Triassic: geologic period from about 250–200 million years ago in which continents drifted apart and the first dinosaurs appeared

Wapiti: also known as elk, one of the largest species within the deer family

Western Interior Seaway: large inland sea that split the continent of North America into two landmasses approximately 100–65 million years ago

wrangler: ranch employee in charge of horses and livestock

Notes & Acknowledgments

My thanks to the editors of the following publications in which the listed poems first appeared, some in different forms.

Move Me Poetry: "Horse Skull Resting in the Endless Grass"; "tree-tops are painting"; "wild peas"; "Katydid"; "One Tenuous Step"
The Power of Poetry: "The Time of Splitting Fishes"
For Awe: "Wildfires"
Ipoetry: "On the Ancient Porch"

This book would not have been possible without the insightful input and support of many friends and family members. I am grateful for my manuscript readers who provided encouragement and comments that helped me see around my blind spots: Cheryl Perrault, Sue Ellen Kuzma, Valerie Anastasio, Liz Sanborn, Jason Fiering, Doyl Fritz, and Tom Bookwalter. Thank you to my wonderful designer and coach, Lindy Gifford, whose creative suggestions and enthusiastic collaboration helped create a book of exceptional beauty and quality, and my copyeditor, Genie Dailey, who ensured I would remember the correct spelling and grammar my parents insisted on in grade school. I am indebted to Mary Eaton and Jeff Way, who understood the value of this project and gave me the unique forum to share my ranch experiences with future dudes. Special thanks to Liz Sanborn, who provided the moving Foreword and some incredible photos from her own visits, and to her family, Scot, Lawrence, and Kiara, for their friendship and for showing my family so much of this beautiful location. A special shout goes out to my daughter, Rosa, who helped me to see things I missed through her photography, and for sharing some of her photos for this book. And of course, to my family—Valerie, Rosa, and Thomas—my gratitude and love for putting up with the challenging process of living with an author deeply in the labor of birthing a first book, and for sharing so many memories together as we continue to explore the extraordinary.

About the Author

SD Stalzer is a writer, photographer, mindfulness practitioner, and serial dude ranch guest. His poetry has appeared in numerous publications, most recently *Move Me Poetry, Know Thyself Heal Thyself, For Awe, The Power of Poetry, Poet Community*, and the upcoming collection, *We Are the Waves*. A classically trained composer of musical pieces for voice, piano, and chamber instruments, SD's poetry focuses on the intersection of human and spiritual experiences, framed through the lenses of rhythm, form, and the natural world. He resides in Massachusetts with his wife, Valerie, their two children, Rosa and Thomas, and their food-oriented circus-trick-performing Chesapeake Bay Retriever, Willa.

www.ingramcontent.com/pod-product-compliance
Lightning Source LLC
Chambersburg PA
CBHW041538120626
46551CB00019B/2755